This book belongs to:

....

Copyright © BPA Publishing Ltd 2020

Author: Pip Reid
Illustrator: Thomas Barnett
Creative Director: Curtis Reid

www.biblepathwayadventures.com

Thank you for supporting Bible Pathway Adventures®. Our adventure series helps parents teach their children more about the Bible in a fun creative way. Designed for the whole family, Bible Pathway Adventures' mission is to help bring discipleship back into homes around the world. The search for truth is more fun than tradition!

The moral rights of author and illustrator have been asserted, this book is copyright.

ISBN: 978-1-98-858516-1

The Exodus

Path to Freedom

*"Your way was through the sea, your path through the great waters;
yet your footprints were unseen." (Psalm 77:19)*

For many years the Hebrew people were slaves in the land of Egypt until God used a man named Moses to free them from Pharaoh, the king of Egypt. Moses led the Hebrews out of Egypt through the harsh valleys of the desert toward the Red Sea. The desert sun was fierce but God had everything figured out.

During the day, God went ahead in a pillar of cloud that kept the Hebrews cool. At night when the desert became cold and dark, He sent a pillar of fire that lit up the sky like fireworks and kept the Hebrews warm. The pillars of cloud and fire showed the Hebrews the way God wanted them to go.

Pharaoh fretted and fumed. He was furious the Hebrews were gone! He gathered all his horses, chariots, and soldiers, and raced across the desert to catch the Hebrews.

Did you know?

Many people believe there are different ways to pronounce God's name. These include Yah, Yahweh, Yahuah, and many others.

When the Hebrews reached the Red Sea, God said to Moses, "Tell the people to camp here. I have hardened Pharaoh's heart so his army will come after you. But I will deal with his soldiers."

Soon, the Egyptian army appeared in the distance. The Hebrews became worried. They said to Moses, "Why have you brought us into the desert to die?" Trapped between the waters of the Red Sea and the Egyptian army, they moaned, "Didn't we tell you to let us stay in Egypt? We were better off as slaves!"

"Don't be so scared," said Moses. "God will save us from Pharaoh. You'll never see the Egyptians again, so calm down and be quiet." As Moses spoke, a cloud appeared between the Egyptian army and the trapped Hebrews. It became as dark as night for the Egyptians but it was as light as day for the Hebrews. Pharaoh and his soldiers could not see a thing!

God gave Moses more instructions. "Reach out the staff and the sea will divide into two parts. Tell the people to walk along the path I will make through the waters. They will reach the other side safely, but the Egyptians will not."

Moses listened to God and lifted up the staff over the sea. That night a strong wind blew until the sea parted. Two giant walls of water stretched as far as the eye could see. The Hebrews stared at the walls of water in front of them. They were taller than the tallest pyramid! They could hardly believe their eyes. God had made a pathway of dry land through the sea for them to walk through.

"Get your animals and follow the path," Moses told the frightened Hebrews. The Hebrews wasted no time. They quickly gathered their animals and rushed across the beach toward the pathway.

Did you know?

Ancient Egyptian chariot wheels and other artifacts have been found at the bottom of the Gulf of Aqaba. This evidence supports the biblical account of the Red Sea Crossing.

Walls of water towered like mountains over the Hebrews. The wind blew and the sea roared. Their hearts pounded with fear as they raced as fast as they could along the pathway through the water.

When Pharaoh saw what was happening, he sent his soldiers to chase after the Hebrews. But God was watching carefully and threw Pharaoh's army into a panic. The horses were terrified, the soldiers got stuck in the sand, and their chariot wheels broke off in the mud. Things did not look good for the Egyptians!

"Their God is fighting for the Hebrews," the Egyptians shouted to each other. "Let's get out of here!" But it was too late. When Moses and the Hebrews finally reached the other side, God said, "Moses, stretch out your hand over the sea and the water will cover the Egyptians."

Moses did as God told him and the giant walls of water came crashing back down over the Egyptian soldiers and their chariots. Pharaoh's army was completely destroyed.

In the wilderness, God made rules for everyone to follow. "If you obey my instructions you won't have the same trouble the Egyptians had," He told the Hebrews.

The Hebrews listened carefully but kept complaining to Moses. "We had a better life in Egypt. You've brought us into this dusty desert to let us starve to death. What shall we eat?"

God said to Moses, "Tell My people I will send them food every day except for one day a week. On that day they shall rest. This will be called the Sabbath. I want to see if they keep My instructions."

From then on when the Hebrew people flung open their tents each morning, small flakes of bread lay scattered on the ground as thick as snowflakes. It was called "manna" and tasted like honey. And each evening before dinner, God sent flocks of birds to the camp for the Hebrews to eat. The birds were called quails and were as tasty as chicken.

Moses led the Hebrews through the desert to a place called Rephidim and set up camp. It didn't take long for the people to start grumbling again. "Moses, we have nothing to drink." Moses sighed and stared at the sky. "God, these people are ready to stone me. What can I do?"

"Strike a rock with the staff," said God. "Water will come out for everyone to drink." Moses obeyed God, and fresh water gushed from the rock.

But the Hebrews' problems were not over. Soon, the bloodthirsty Amalekites appeared on the horizon. They had heard of Egypt's horrible plagues and the death of Pharaoh's army. When they saw the Hebrews, they said, "It's time to conquer Egypt!" They sharpened their knives, ready for battle.

Joshua picked the strongest men he could find and led them into battle. As long as Moses held up his arms, the Hebrews won; but when he put down his arms, the Amalekites started winning. When Moses arms grew tired, Aaron and Hur stood beside him and held his arms above his head. With God on their side, the Hebrews fought their enemies and won, and the Amalekites disappeared into the desert.

Moses was eager to continue the journey through the desert. He was back in a familiar land - after all, he had lived in the wilderness before he left to rescue God's people. The Hebrews listened to Moses, packed up their tents, and marched toward a mountain called Sinai.

Imagine everyone in your family going camping for forty years. Would you all get along all the time? It was the same for the Hebrews. Moses tried to sort out everyone's problems. But there were so many that his ears got tired just listening to them all. Luckily Jethro, Moses' father-in-law, had an idea.

"Moses, you'll wear yourself out listening to everyone's problems. Your job is to lead the people. Let other men take care of the day-to-day matters." Even though Moses was the boss, he listened to what Jethro told him. He chose wise men and put them in charge of the people.

Did you know?

A shofar is a special ceremonial trumpet made from a ram's horn. It is used to announce special events on God's calendar.

In the third month after the Hebrews left Egypt, they arrived at Mount Sinai. God said to Moses, "Tell everyone to wash their clothes and get ready. In three days I will come down onto the mountain."

On the morning of the third day, a thick dark cloud appeared over the top of Mount Sinai. Thunder and lightning crashed and rumbled across the sky. The sound of a heavenly shofar echoed across the desert.

Moses led the Hebrews out of the camp to meet God. With their legs shaking like jelly, they stared up at the smoke rising from the mountain. "What is happening to us?" they cried. They were very afraid of the presence of God.

The sound of the shofar grew louder and louder. A mighty voice boomed across the desert. "I am the Lord your God who brought you out of Egypt and freed you from slavery." The Hebrews fell on their faces, their hearts pounding with fear. God's instructions to His people Israel were about to be revealed.

With a flash of lightning and a crack of thunder, God spoke these Words to the people.

1. "You will have no other gods but Me."

2. "You will not make any statues or pictures to worship Me."

3. "You will not take My name lightly."

4. "You will keep the Sabbath and set it apart for Me."

5. "You will respect your father and mother."

6. "You will not murder."

7. "You will not commit adultery."

8. "You will not steal."

9. "You will not lie about other people."

10. "You will not desire other people's possessions."

Filled with fear, the Israelites covered their ears. "From now on, you tell us what God says," they said to Moses. "If God speaks to us again, we will die." "Don't be afraid," said Moses. "God has come to test you and make sure you obey Him, so you will not sin."

While the Israelites stared up at the smoking mountain, God continued giving Moses His instructions. Then, Moses built an altar and set up twelve large stones, one for each of the tribes of Israel. The people gathered certain animals and burned them on the altar to show God that they would obey His instructions.

Moses walked up the mountain into the cloud. For forty days, God taught him all about His covenant so Moses could teach the Israelites His ways. Moses listened carefully to everything God told him, and wrote God's Words on two stone tablets to show the people.

Down in the camp, the Israelites became restless. "We haven't seen Moses for weeks. He could be dead for all we know." They came up with a silly plan. "Let us make God in our own image," they told Aaron. Without the support of his brother Moses, Aaron wasn't sure what to do. He wanted to please the people. Glancing nervously up at the mountain, he said, "Bring me all your gold jewelry."

Aaron melted down the gold jewelry and made it into the shape of a calf. Then he built another stone altar, and after the people gave a peace offering, they had a party that lasted all day and all night.

God watched what was happening down in the camp. He said, "Moses, the people are worshipping a gold calf. Perhaps I should wipe them out and start again with you." Moses begged God not to kill the Israelites. "Don't destroy your people. Remember your promise to make them a great nation." God heard Moses' cries and was pleased. He had allowed the Israelites' bad behavior to test Moses' heart. He turned His thoughts away from judging the people.

But Moses still wasn't happy with the Israelites' behavior. Tucking the stone tablets under his arms, he raced down the mountain back to the camp. When he saw the people worshiping a false god, he threw the tablets on the ground, smashing them into tiny pieces.

"Why did you make this calf?" Moses asked Aaron. Aaron hung his head in shame. "You know what the people are like. The people became afraid so I took their gold and threw it in the fire, and out came this calf…" Moses ordered the calf to be melted down and ground into powder. Then, pouring the powder into the water, he ordered everyone to drink it to punish them for what they had done.

Moses pleaded with God to spare the people. But God still punished them for making the calf. He sent a plague to remind the Israelites that He was angry. Then with His own finger, God wrote His Words on a new set of stone tablets.

While the Israelites were in the wilderness, God told Moses to build a special tent called a tabernacle where the people could worship Him. Nobody had built a tent like this before, so God told them what to do.

The Israelites listened carefully and made pieces of furniture to go inside the tent. The most important piece they made was a wooden box covered in gold. Inside it held God's Words, which was His covenant with His people. The box was known as the Ark of the Covenant.

God put Aaron in charge of the tabernacle and called him the High Priest. As part of this special assignment, Aaron and his sons wore different clothes and helped the people worship God.

When the Israelites finished making the special tent, a large cloud descended over the area and the tabernacle was filled with God's presence. From that time on, whenever the cloud moved, the Israelites knew it was time to pack up their tents and continue their journey.

God knew His people had learned to worship false gods while they were slaves in Egypt. "Do not live how the Egyptians live," He told them. "They disobey Me and worship false gods, and this is not good. Teach the people to celebrate My Feasts. These are My special meeting times and dress rehearsals for My people."

Moses explained God's Feasts to the Israelites. He told them about the Passover and Feasts of Unleavened Bread, First Fruits, and Pentecost. Then he explained the Day of Trumpets, the Day of Atonement, the Feast of Tabernacles, and the Last Great Day.

"These are God's special times and dates," said Moses. "They teach us about His promises and plans. He wants us to honor and remember them forever." People began to learn God's ways instead of the ways of Egypt, and God was pleased.

The Israelites continued their journey through the wilderness. As they neared the land of Canaan, God said to Moses, "Send twelve men out to explore this land I have promised you."

Moses chose a spy from each of the twelve tribes of Israel, including two men named Caleb and Joshua. "I want to know what Canaan looks like," Moses told the men. "Are the people strong? What kind of cities do they live in? If you dare, take some fruit from their vineyards, then come back and tell me everything!"

For forty days the spies explored the mighty land of Canaan. But they were in for a big surprise. There were fearsome giants as tall as cedar trees. The men had never seen such enormous people! Trembling with fear, they raced back to the camp as fast as their wobbly legs could carry them.

Back at the camp the spies waved a giant bunch of grapes in front of Moses. "The land really does flow with milk and honey. But the men are fierce. We even saw the bloodthirsty Amalekites! There's no way we can live there."

Caleb and Joshua, who were much braver than the other men, spoke up. "What are you talking about? The land is amazing. Let's go and conquer it now!"

"We can't attack those people," said the frightened men. "Did you see the giants? They're much bigger and stronger than we are. We looked like grasshoppers compared to them. Are you crazy?"

Caleb and Joshua had great faith in God and pleaded with the Israelites. "We've got nothing to worry about. God is on our side. He'll give us the land He has promised."

The Israelites had not learned to trust God, and they refused to believe Joshua and Caleb. They moaned and groaned, and wept all night. "We wish we had died in the wilderness. Why is God bringing us into this land to kill us? Let's choose another leader and go back to Egypt."

God was angry at their lack of faith. "How long will I have to put up with these people grumbling about Me? They never stop. If that's how they feel, none of them will see this land!"

To punish them for their lack of faith, God made the Israelites live in the wilderness until all the adults died. Only their children could enter the new land.

Did you know?

When Moses and the Israelites left Egypt, they took the bones of Joseph with them. (Exodus 13:19)

Moses must have trusted God because leading the Israelites for forty years in the wilderness wasn't easy. He got tired at their lack of faith. They fought lots of battles and rebelled against God many times. And they kept on complaining. "We don't have any water to drink."

Moses had heard enough. He leapt to his feet and grabbed the staff. "Listen here, you rebels! Are God and I supposed to bring you water from this rock?" He smacked the rock with the staff and water gushed out.

God was not pleased with Moses' behavior. "Moses, did you bring water forth from the rock? Because you stole My glory you will not go into the land I have given My people."

Moses clasped his head in his hands. "What have I done?" he cried. He had led the people through the wilderness for forty years, and now he wasn't allowed to go into the Promised Land. He pleaded with God, saying, "Please, let me go across the Jordan River to see the land." But God did not change His mind.

Finally, when Moses was 120 years old, God told him it was time for Joshua to take charge of the Israelites. Moses gathered everyone together and reminded them of God's instructions, saying, "You have seen everything God has done for you. Obey His instructions and life will be better."

Moses left the plains of Moab and climbed to the top of Mount Nebo. At the top of the mountain God showed Moses all the land He had promised His people, who were now the twelve tribes of Israel. "This land I swore that I would give to Abraham, Isaac, and Jacob. I promise I will give it to your descendants."

Even though Moses didn't enter the Promised Land, God was pleased with him. He loved His humble servant. When Moses died, God Himself buried Moses in the land of Moab. Since then, no one has ever shown the mighty power or performed the awesome deeds that Moses did in the sight of all Israel.

It was now time for Joshua and the Israelites to take the Promised Land!

THE END

TEST YOUR KNOWLEDGE!

(Match the question with the answer at the bottom of the page)

QUESTIONS

Who led the Israelites out of Egypt? ....

Who guided the Israelites through the wilderness? ....

Which army chased after the Israelites? ....

How did Moses command the sea to divide so the Israelites could cross to the other side? ....

Which sea did the Israelites cross through to escape the Egyptians? ....

How did God stop the Egyptians chasing the Israelites across the sea? ....

What happened to the Egyptian army? ....

What did the Israelites do when they reached the other side of the sea? ....

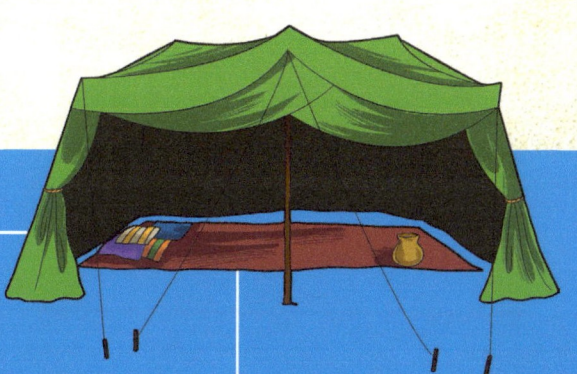

ANSWERS

1. Moses
2. The Angel of God in a pillar of cloud or fire
3. The Egyptian army
4. He lifted up his rod and stretched his hand over the sea
5. The Red Sea
6. He made the wheels of their chariots break
7. They drowned in the sea
8. Sang a song to Yahweh

Complete the Word Search Puzzle

MOSES   CALF
HEBREWS   ARK
PHARAOH   SINAI
TABERNACLE   JOSHUA
SPIES   QUAIL

```
T M J W E J B Q H H
A P B W P O G U E P
B D H H M S B A B K
E W M A R H J I R Y
R G V F R U A L E M
N A R K P A Y N W O
A P H G J D O L S S
C S I N A I Z H S E
L F Z Z N C A L F S
E U B B S P I E S U
```

Bible Pathway Adventures®

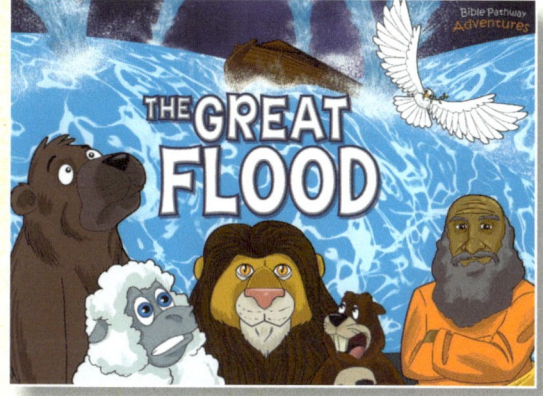

Birth of the King
Betrayal of the King
The Risen King
Swallowed by a Fish
The Chosen Bride
Saved by a Donkey
Thrown to the Lions
Facing the Giant
Samson Mighty Warrior
Sold into Slavery
The Great Flood
Shipwrecked!
Escape from Egypt

Discover more Bible Pathway Adventures' Bible stories!

Check out Bible Pathway Adventures' Activity Books

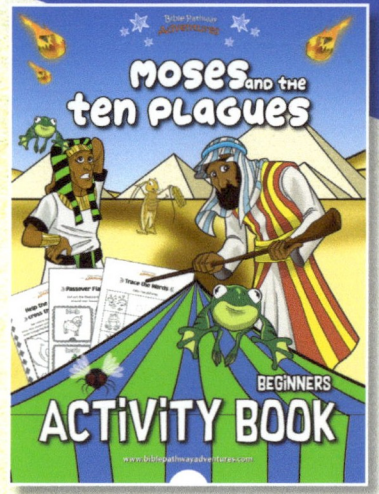
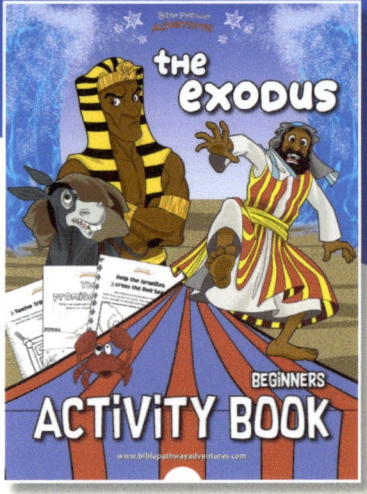

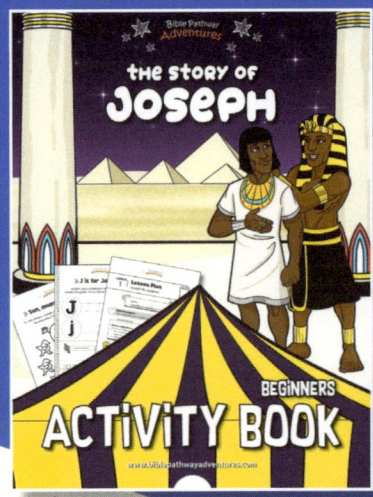
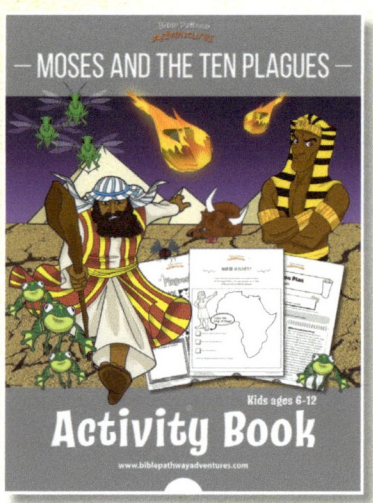

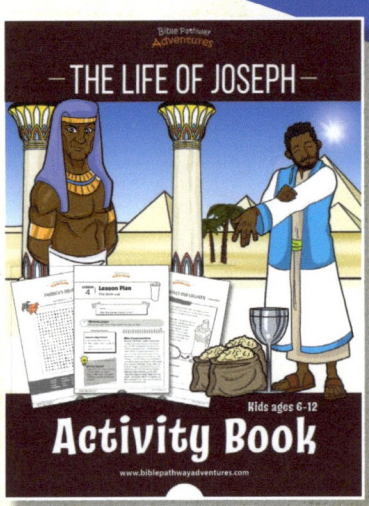

GO TO

www.biblepathwayadventures.com

www.ingramcontent.com/pod-product-compliance
Lightning Source LLC
Chambersburg PA
CBHW040318100526

44583CB00004BB/140